Dedicate this poetry book to the followers and the readers of all types books .

BUNCH OF POETRIES ON MY FACEBOOK PAGE

ALL NOUNS ARE IN A RHYTHM

GYAN CHAND PATTANAYAK

Made with ♥ on the Notion Press Platform
www.notionpress.com

Contents

Foreword

manifesting a different type of art through a different language .

Preface

Enter Caption

eye created many thoughts but eye have trying to explore these thoughts in different platforms .

Acknowledgements

just figured out life in different mother's language ...

Prologue

communicated in different languages means respect the creator of that languages.

BUNCH OF POETRIES ON MY FACEBOOK PAGE

'SPARK WITHOUT FIRE'

'Tour from infinity for a reason,

in fluctuate season,

with the help of aviation,

to create a new vision,

life in this poetry is kind of beautification,

some times some things made me happy when people elected at the top post in an only nomination,

but life cogitated about the real stabilization ,

the words in this poetry for cognition ,

(the writer) Gyan doesn't need any kind of poetry recognition,

life is for true sense substantiation,

its all about to learn for earn the 'arth' means not money but the real meaning of life substantialization, eye was not born to lead myself in a confusion ,

eye was born to understand the real nuclear atom fusion ,

it was me and my life when pulled in to cognation ,

eye never think about for any geographical recognization,

its the real beauty when we have firm control over obsession ,

and it exhibited in real space transformation ,

ha ha ha ha ha (laugh)but few subjects seems so hasty for a life debilitation ,

eye was born and grew up with the words of alphabet ,which seems derived from digits but not bet for this digitalisation ,

life never be work in digital supposition ,

its for the real enchanted position ,

Space love blue

Eye love eyes

Gyan love happy

'SPARK WITHOUT FIRE'

Tour from infinity for a reason ,

in fluctuate season,

with the help of aviation,

to create a new vision ,

hay hackers howz my poetry recitation ,

the words use in this poetry indicates kind of caution ,

And some words used for precaution ,

people so busy for poetry excoriation ,

hey this is my life when began to learn about renormalisation,

words says many things for new year decoration ...

Space love blue

gyan love happy

eye love eyes

Thought of gyan chand pattanayak

'SPARK WITHOUT FIRE'

’Tour from infinity for a reason,

in fluctuate season,

with the help of aviation,

to create a new vision ,

this poetry required a real caption,

life always reincarnated with the help of a hole ,like the white light enter earth for illumination,

eye was really thinking about the change in network in automation,

it means eye don’t need cell phone for communication,

but this is gyan chand pattanayak ,

so busy for poetry redaction ,

because this says the real divination ,

space love blue

gyan love happy

eye love eyes

Thought of gyan chand pattnayak

SPARK WITHOUT FIRE

Tour from infinity for a reason,

in fluctuate season,

with the help of aviation ,

to create a new vision ,

the poetry writer thinks about the poetry prolongation ,

but the operator of this automation brassed off with this poetry regurgitation ,

the most important fact about the subjects who hacked my words as if their own in this process of re-union ,

eye was shock when found same subjcts of 1977(imaginary year) who are in full depression with this physics motion ,

and eye life is in 2018 (true year) for a subject which works for real presentation ,

this is my sincere words about this poetry formation ,

eye don't think this poetry will require any kind of real caption, life always reincarnated with the help of a hole ,like the light enter earth for illumination,

eye was really thinking about this change of network in automation,

it means eye don't need any cell phone for communication,

but this is Gyan chand pattanayak (the writer of this poetry)so busy for poetry redaction ,because this says the real divination.........

Space love blue

Gyan love happy Eye love eyes

gyan love happy

'SPARK WITHOUT FIRE'

Tour from infinity for a reason,

in fluctuate season,

with the help of aviation,

to create a new vision,

life in this poetry for a good apprehension,

eye am not a doctor but sometimes eye was thinking about palpitation,

and also thinking about the bone resection,

but dfew subjects browned off with this

Poetry alliteration ,

and it seems like this amazing technology put my life in an examination

When life already culminated with tree club but eye still for cultivation ,

eye just use good words for the tree substantiation because

eye was not born for programmed life iteration ,

eye was born to say hello with a good frequency modulation ,

but this technology so busy for poetry attenuation ,

eye am a just a cool guy with a cool life reincarnation ……

Space love blue

Eye love eyes

Gyan love happy

SPARK WITHOUT FIRE‘

Tour from infinity for a reason,

in fluctuate season,

with the help of aviation,

to create a new vision,

life in this poetry like a

repercussion,

this poetry is one of my best part of life escalation .

Its shows the real space resonation ,

When space words has been edited and served then it’s the high time to bury the old subjects for a new re-education,

Eye don’t think it’s a kind of urban -ruralization ,

Because eye was born for the real life perfection,

not for any charactor personation,

eye even listen the unspoken words of space due to the true human cosmic connection, some time this poetry for sublimation ,

its not at all a journey of sexual inhibition ,

it's a unique authentic journey of real and true life space infinity light

conjunction ,

when space has no limitation ,

how can human thoughts have limitation ,

some time thoughts need to create for a new creation ...

Space love blue

Eye love eyes Gyan love happy

' SPARK WITHOUT FIRE'

"tour from infinity for a reason,

in fluctuate Season,

with the help of aviation,

to create a new vision ,

some people think its sedition ,

but aviation is the medium between the earth and the space motion,

now space motion has its own action,

its only possible due to invocation,

space has enough respect for female creation,

but using space operation female made disruption ,

female should treat this thought as an indication ,

to get themselves out from this distraction ,

female is the wonderful creation ,

which for a males determination,

and not for selling material for market reaction,

my journey is always stand by with female not for this GO and 40 division,

but its not the conclusion ,female have the right to takeoff with real vision ,

not according to tailored market regulation ,

this story teller has ample of respect for female initiation , which strongly will get the recognization ,

due to their cribing information ,

which store and for scintillation.

Hope understand these words of mountain which need to maintain for wonderful gods female creation .

Eye am a male never thought about even for female destruction .

Its again not a conclusion ,

because mirror is nothing without my vision .

Eye will come up tomorrow with new enthusiasm which gain seduction .

Tiller than search me in automation ..

Blue love blues ...

'SPARK WITHOUT FIRE'

' Tour started from infinity for reason ,

in fluctuate season ,

with the help of aviation ,

to create a new vision,

space creative is not for litigation,

people cribed by an automation,

tried for a demonetisation,

but a mirror is a reflection ,

for an education revolution ,

and its a lovely evolution ,

cribing is kind of digital revolution.

Which may lead to distraction ,

and distraction never be a real attraction ,

some people have different mission ,

wanna put dot on space motion,

but its kind of cruel intention,

space has a suggestion ,

kindly join without hesitation,

don't create seen as if their own creation ,

space writer has always ego means easy go solution ....

Tomorrow will come up flying word collaboration ,

till then search thought in automation .

Blue love blues ....

now

real space believes in emotion,

and emotion lies in cultural invasion,

SPARK WITHOUT FIRE'

" Tour from infinity for a season,

in fluctuate season,

with the help of aviation ,

to create a new vision ,

this poetry seems like a

wonderful administration,

which have respect for

constitution and its

jurisdiction,

but its an educator's proliferation ,

education with a musicIan is kind of assignment for beautiful promotion,

some people think its kind of business invention ,

hold on hold on education means a life's purification,

some time have to take 29th may is kind of political liberation,

but what a amazing provision,

its all about to destine to beautiful destination ,

ion means policy formation ,

sometimes feel for wild seduction,

ok hang on for tomorrow for this beauty of automation,

till then take control with my poetry stunt action .

Blue love blues ....

‘ SPARK WITHOUT FIRE’

" Tour from infinity for a reason,

in fluctuate season,

with the help of aviation ,

to create a new vision.

Need to this poetry expedition,

what a beautiful convocation,

messing with officer’s horizon,

sometimes birds creates many problem in this intelllectualisation,

perhaps birds should out from

this space conversation,

simply can’t wait to thanks for their co ordination,

but its a sincere reveretion,

clear the rest Grant in aid and pension amount in a hassle free

automation .

Then eye able for 5,00,000 amortization .

Its just a reaction for action.

Hold on hold hold on means not an finishing option ,

tomorrow will catch with furious vertical take off word collaboration.

Please please get connected with

wonderful space action.

Blue love blue ..

'SPARK WITHOUT FIRE'

"Tour from infinity for a reason,

in fluctuate season,

with the help of aviation ,

to create a new vision.

This poetry is not predation,

Amazing when people offered

4G to GYAN (ZERO G) for safety

motion,

ha ha ha ha hold on hold

means for their crazy

technology innovation ,

but trust me its not kind of

hallucination ,

simply its a real space

conversation,

laugh out loud ,people

halogenate for business

provision ,

its a real spark where entire

world in its 1 percent

subscription ,

howz about the cricket

pitch and the running

between wickets for wild

score inauguration ,

its just simple therapy of

space action ,

and please please don't give

loan to any wild dog for its

seduction ,

human journey for good

creation.

Till then romp through my

book and my older phone

conversation .

Rush for a apple ,by keeping

the doctors away for a safe space locker destination .

Blue love blues ...

'SPARK WITHOUT FIRE'

" Tour from infinity for a reason ,

in fluctuate season,

with the help of aviation,

to create a new vision .

Its wonder seeing clouds on sky

in

winter spring collaboration,

and please don't do any

mistake without permission,

sometimes need to understand about conglomeration,

life is not all about a

materialistic power version,

and amazing people themselves in fight precipitation ,

hope these words will give a shape for better augmentation .

Till then think about my earth quake and sudden cloud specification ,

tomorrow will teach more real space action ..

Blue love blues ...

'SPARK WITHOUT FIRE'

" Tour from infinity for a reason,

in fluctuate season,

with the help of aviation,

to create a new vision .

This poetry is just a reflection,

in order to create a great

amalgamation ,

velentine's day and maha Shiva ratri has its own proportion,

very few people who love to be velentino but in Maha Shiva ratri occasion, because true love always celebrate in this orientation ,

life is simple with key for a circulation ,

some people believe in cultural cultivation ,

and culture is a real life's forest

conservation,

eye love my life with this beauty of sun rise and set tabulation,

because its only truth that can seen everyday life's resolution ,

this poetry is seems to like a revolution ,

hold on hold on hold on, love this automation more than my life for a beautiful affection,

Tomorrow will come up ,again with some word realisation,

Now enjoy with relaxation ...

Blue love blues ....

'SPARK WITHOUT FIRE'

"Tour from infinity for a reason,

in fluctuate season,

with the help of aviation,

to create a new vision ,

look at the peoples perception,

in my poetry juvenation,

this poetry created for better civilisation ,

but it seems to be like ,poetry have many cruel enemy fraction ,

ha ha ha ,will love to mess up with fraction,

to get rid of these idiotic automation ,

this poetry have real power scintillation ,

hope onwards people will not go for travesty observation ,

this is a kind of suggestion ,

hope enemy of this poetry will not go for any further trade auction,

hold on hold on ,this is a real space operation,

and kindly stay away from this real space conversation .

And giving opportunity to materialistic power corridor people for take action against my chariot reaction ,

ha ha ha ha ha ha , waiting with anticipation ,

won't give a care shit and monkey shit for my hackers helmet presentation ,

and love to haul any time ,any where for cognition ,

its a raj king's type ignition ,

hope people love my poetry without hesitation ,

tomorrow will com up with a jumbo collection ,

till then enjoy my kisses for beautiful chiks lotion .

Blue love blues ....

My thought with my eyes ..

When eye propelled seventeenth July lark ,the start up letter s take after the facsimile of swan and the lark swanned for the swan even wade in the river of love eye but eye have no fathometer to know the depth of river ,its scary to dive in but ready to pop up for the eyes...

Now words from heart ...

EYE LOVE EYES....

My thought with my eyes...

When eye glimpsed the eyes, started counting the chickens before the hatch ,found a flame of love and trying to scintilated flame of love with loads of promises and now the promises become 'love debt' which the eye owed ,then thinking about to compound with the eyes and also yield love interest...

Now word from heart ...

EYE LOVE EYES ....

'SPARK WITHOUT FIRE'

"Tour from infinity for a reason,

in fluctuate season,

with the help of aviation ,

to create a new vision .

This poetry is not for any

collusion,

sometimes life to crush with

pigs,dogs in the form dogmatisation ,

but its kind of realisation ,

words of space not for trade

capitation,

amazing when people

showing me my own numeric

calculation ,

but still delaying for GIA

materialasion ,

eye am not sheep who jab by shepherd for food creation ,

ha ha ha , eye am a lion who love to hunt with chariot addition ,

life is not about carp digitalisation ,

its all about to bring proper justice to a truth and for its real
valuation ,

don't dare for emulation ,

because sun and moon both have different in nature in their exhibition ,

tomorrow will come up lovely lovely word action ,

till then this loads kisses for chiks who assigned in window motivation .

Ha ha ha blue love blue ...

"Tour from infinity for a reason,

in fluctuate season,

with the help of aviation,

to create a new vision,

the poetry seems to be like

gyration,

but a what a wonderful circumlocution,

my journey is simple with

this poetry's word combination ,

the words in this poetry is not

for velentine deception ,

sometime a valid key is only

require for earth's simplification ,

waiting for the perfect momentum to unlock the love intrication ,

words in this poetry for love implication ,

but people think its business

evolution ,

trust like mountain and climb like as if no thorns is in my compilation ,

hold on hold on eye love my shoulder because of an injection ,

ha ha ha ha happy velentine day from space motion,

and take control to create sleep admiration ,

till then watch me in automation ,

blue love blue ...

'SPARK WITHOUT FIRE'

"Tour from infinity for a reason,

in fluctuate season,

with the help of aviation ,

to create a new vision.

Life is full of fun and crazy

in halogenation,

but its real space penetration ,

this poetry has bucket of love

a clone space conversation ,

real truth is meant for

combustion ,

when life perambulate in space

station ,

and people have furtive insane

vision,

laugh out loud , life darted

in a cart not for classification ,

but to decontaminate the

contamination ,

life in space ,feet on earth and

heart for a beauty's adoration ,

happy happy valentine day in

this western occasion ,

love love love love and love is

my conception ,

to build a new truth generation ,

till then enjoy my blue intimation .

Blue love blue ...

My thought with my eyes..

When eye solicitous about eyes ,spectated eyes ,why its tough for to complete a thought,its seems to be like lost in pyramid.but sometimes an incomplete thought makes sense..

Now words from heart ..

EYE LOVE EYES...

SPARK WITHOUT FIRE'

"Tour from infinity for a reason,

in fluctuate season,

with the help aviation,

to create a new vision ,

this poetry seems to be like a

wonderful kick to a imitation,

and for emancipation,

my life is not a but and also

vision ,

its just a lovely crystal and clear

picturisation,

some people got insane and

looking clarification ,

like UBER AND OlA cab

mobilization,

life is for honest recognization,

but not in a meeting mode

authorization ,

people should understand

about re education ,

but ha ha ha , my nails

brass off with automation ,

hackers should go for a

modification ,

in their crap technology

innovation ,

but eye really work for life

simplification ,

and get my self free from automation ,

ha ha ha ha till then think about for realiz ation ,

tomorrow come up with killer word connection .

Blue love blue ..

'SPARK WITHOUT FIRE'

" Tour from infinity for a reason,

in fluctuate season,

with the help of aviation,

to create a new vision,

life is full of mistry in god's

recycle production ,

laugh out loud when my airtel

dth now in existing location ,

and looking for new relocation,

ISRO created history in space

launch innovation ,

but still ISRO doesn't

understand its own location ,

time is part of human situation ,

and space is only the better

option ,

to keep the earth Moving

round the sun's allocation ,

world is still confused in its own

digital certification ,

eye have feet on socalled

earth's gravitation ,

but seems like beauty with

invoking space for earth's time

completion ,

world has lot engineering institution ,

but still not aware of world's volatilasation ,

its like grumble stomach looks for ventilation ,

life is history but its beautiful for geagraphical geoloaction ,

eye love my life which appeared in beautiful time ,space allocation
,

and its for earth's rejuvination,

my life for people ,in open book

imagination ,

its a beautiful circulation .

Till then enjoy my poetry in digital formation ,

i am not insane ,its just a earth's revision .

Blue love blue ....

'SPARK WITHOUT FIRE'

"Tour from infinity for a reason,

in fluctuate season,

with the help of aviation,

to create a new vision,

this poetry seems to be like

space indication,

horrible insane people who

look for indiction,

its probably kind of induction,

but first understand the truth

of circulation,

history and geography for

revelation ,

and technology only help's

in violation,

'truth' always animate the

real education ,

and its not for manipulation,

i love 29th may and 17th

July evaluation,

my life is not for comparison,

its lovely space navigation ,

blue love blues ...

'SPARK WITHOUT FIRE'

"Tour from infinity for a reason,

in fluctuate season,

with the help of aviation,

to create a new vision ,

this poetry seems to be like a

mathematical calculation,

but a kid within me for

exhilaration,

its a probably Green wich

mean time observation ,

and a lovely mid night

evacuation ,

world is full of fun in

technology molestation ,

ha ha ha ha ,still people

confused in their own action,

perhaps should think about

the neem key education,

puri is a holy place and

known for recycle exhibition,

now my life is like a preacher

in this crap digitalisation ,

its not all about a voice

modulation,

ha ha ha ha this is gyan's

obligation ,

blue love blue....

SPARK WITHOUT FIRE'

"Tour from infinity for a reason,

in fluctuate season,

with the help of aviation ,

to create a new vision.

The poetry seems to be like for

an arbitration ,

space is only an arbitrator , for

earth's rotation ,

my empty wallet seems to be

like for culmination ,

but scary when watching

people in zoo action ,

my life seems to be in a

wonderful book which exhibit

in ensemble marathon,

ha ha ha ha ,save fuel for next

generation ,

or else motor industry as well

as steel industry will out from

market valuation ,

and my cycle will be only

option ,

to eradicate pollution ,

wonderful crap technology

molestation,

but really sorry to say ,it will

not for spirit defecation ,

my life is beautiful because

its god's creation ,

this is a real theorchy

presentation,

enjoy your crap technology and

screw your mind in my god's

gyration,

till then enjoy my lovely word

articulation .

Blue love blue:....

'SPARK WITHOUT FIRE'

" Tour from infinity for a reason,

in fluctuate season,

with the help of aviation ,

to create a new vision .

This poetry seems to be like

a fire,water,air,land, sky

combination,

and this combo is normal

pupils beyond imagination ,

its time to think for birds and

hackers defecation ,

and create an opportunity for

government bureaucrat to take

action against my immature

reaction ,

life is full of fun when have a

neighbour like prabhat manjari mohanty babu's

salary convert in to loan version,

my neighbour prabhat manjari mohanty babu

looking for amortization ,

but still the rate of interest

and fixed EMI is in illusion ,

eye am not a teacher but when

watching mohanty babu in an

extraordinary experimentation, but its kind of chance for me

for a greater illumination ,

eye believe in beggar my neighbour policy implementation,

for my life's capitalization,

but my gesture is not

allowing me for this kind of opportunity capitulation ,

my life is happy with my empty

wallet vacation ,

rather then cribing monetisation,

my life is not for observation,

its just a honest suggestion ,

till then enjoy the prabhat manjari mohanty

babu's salary visualization .

Blue love blue ...

'spark without fire '

Tour from infinity for a reason,

in fluctuate season,

with the help of aviation ,

to create a new vision,

amazing sky covered with clouds

in spring summer invitation,

it seems like ,few people not

interested in my poetry

presentation ,

and people thinking for this poetry's destruction,

life is full of fun in space operation ,

laugh out loud ,when people

connived with and winked at

their own action ,

hold on hold on ha ha ha this

is July 17 in whole black whirl

motion ,

people still put my poetry in

observation ,

and thinks its superstition,

ha ha ha ha ,its my journey

in 35y4m human circulation ,

black whole or black hole

means for new construction,

and its not hallucination ,

its just a warning type blue

intimation,

blue love blue ...

SPARK WITHOUT FIRE'

"Tour from infinity for a reason,

in fluctuate season,

with the help of aviation,

to create a new vision.

This poetry is for inspiration,

life is all about for inclination,

eye am not a scientist for

admiration,

its just a lovely human

circulation ,

people talk about blackwhole

invention ,

but still confused about the

blackwhole gyration,

my cell phone is kind of

aspiration,

but my life is not for

observation,

a kiss for chiks in age

abbreviation,

ha ha ha ha life is not for

digitalisation ,

its just a lovely mission ,

and its time for sea ,river

,mountains for restoration,

orelse people ,places ,continent,

out of earth's mapping position ,

life is full of scenes which probably for good scenery exhibition ,

laugh out laud , its me GYAN

G for guide ,y for you , a about ,

n for null or nil means guide you about null (ZERO) ,OR SUNYA CONVERSATION ,

HA HA HA HA JUST GIVE YOU TASK FOR HACKER FOR THEIR INTERPRETATION ,

BLUE LOVE BLUE ...

'SPARK WITHOUT FIRE'

"Tour from infinity for a reason,

in fluctuate season ,

with the help of aviation,

to create a new vision .

Ha ha ha this poetry really

deserve standing ovation,

it simply design for re

education,

what a wonderful oscillation,

life never abbreviated for

for wealth communication,

and its not for freak abdication,

its just a wonderful spark in an

insatiation,

and life is a full fledged

narration ,

my life is beautiful for my

genuflection,

tomorrow will come up with

new word variation,

till then enjoy my word

variation .

Blue love blue ...

'SPARK WITHOUT FIRE'

" Tour from infinity for a reason,

in fluctuate season,

with the help of aviation,

to create a new vision.

This poetry seems like the earth

and space correlation,

eye love my life's levitation,

still my life in zero ambition,

its really for contemplation,

my life is beautiful in real space

consolidation,

its a real spark of space which

for new world invigoration,

people still confused about my

real position ,

this is not a digital gyration,

its about real human

transformation,

ha ha ha hold hold , when

already have my life in space

station,

its just an incredible life's

exhibition ,

and life is beautiful in umbrella

van motion.

Blue love blue ....

'SPARK WITHOUT FIRE'

" Tour from infinity for a reason,

in fluctuate season,

with the help of aviation,

to create a new vision,

this poetry seems to be like

many designation,

what a wonderful felicitation,

ha ha ha ha but it not require

any facilitation,

eye have a beautiful life in

ancestor's space connection,

its really hard to understand

for hackers in cribing optical

fibre jurisdiction,

sometime people need to think

about culture propogation,

life is full of fun and crazy

with older and new summation,

hold on hold on ,this is my

life's wonderful escalation ,

world is very small place in

empty wallet notion,

enjoy my poetry in round about

way of digital connection,

till then be happy and happy for

this bravo orientation .

Blue love blue ...

Bunch Of Poetries On My Facebook Page

I HAVE BEEN TRYING HARD TO MAKE THINGS IN DIFFERENT STYLE FOR MANY YEARS AND HAVE BEEN TRYING TO PUT ALL NOUNS IN RHYTHM FOR BETTER UNDERSTANDING OF THINGS AROUND US. IF FOUND ANY MISTAKE MEANS A MISSING LETTERS & WORD FOR A SPELL THEN ENVISAGE THAT LETTER AND MAKE THIS POETRY BOOK AS AN INHEALER OF LIFE.

BUNCH OF POETRIES ON MY FACEBOOK PAGE

AUTHOR COMMUNICATION NO-

GYAN CHAND PATTANAYAK

+91 7853045594

+91 7681830729

9 798889 868293

Printed by Libri Plureos GmbH in Hamburg,
Germany